Original title:
The Sea's Memory

Copyright © 2025 Creative Arts Management OÜ
All rights reserved.

Author: Lorenzo Barrett
ISBN HARDBACK: 978-1-80587-449-2
ISBN PAPERBACK: 978-1-80587-919-0

## Heritage of the Tides

Waves laugh and dance, such cheeky sprites,
Carrying whispers of curious kites.
Seagulls chuckle with each salty breeze,
As crabs in the sand do as they please.

Old fish share tales of long-ago pranks,
With shells as their mugs, at the ocean banks.
Starfish giggle, they surely have sass,
Counting their friends who just might be grass.

## Beneath the Glistening Surface

Bubbles float up, they puff and they pop,
Fish in bright colors do a flip-flop.
Jellyfish jellyfish, a wobbly show,
With smiles and winks as they drift to and fro.

Octopuses dancing with many a leg,
While clams just sit there, snug as a peg.
Oh, what a party in depths so profound,
Underwater laughter, a joy that's unbound.

## A Maritime Mosaic

Buoyant boats bobbing on waves of delight,
With fishermen sharing a joke in the night.
Mermaids gossip over seashells so bright,
While dolphins leap up, quite the dazzling sight.

Barnacles brag about who's got the most,
As turtles chime in, raising a toast.
Pirates chuckle, their treasure map tossed,
As the waves give a wink, oh, the joy not lost!

## The Call of the Siren's Past

Sirens are singing with melodies sweet,
And fish all wiggle to the catchy beat.
Anemones sway, with charisma and flair,
While shrimp do the cha-cha without a care.

Shells hold their breath, all clamored in glee,
For each tiny wave brings gags and esprit.
The ocean's a circus, a whimsical show,
With laughs and a splash, it's all fun down below!

## The Tidal Echo

Waves laugh loudly as they crash,
Salt sprays dance, making a splash.
Seagulls argue over a fry,
While crabs crawl by with a curious eye.

Beach balls bounce like joyful stars,
As surfers ride their liquid parts.
The tide whispers jokes from afar,
And shells giggle, hiding in jars.

## Reflections on the Water's Edge

Footprints slip like they're in a race,
Chasing reflections that vanish without trace.
A fish winks at me from below,
While I wave back like a star of the show.

My hat flies off in a sea breeze chase,
As sunbathers laugh at my silly face.
The tide rolls in with a ticklish tease,
Leaving me grinning, whispering 'please!'

## A Journey Through the Blue

I float on a raft, a pirate's delight,
While dolphins giggle in the bright sunlight.
Seashells gossip as I pass them by,
One claimed to be part of a giant's tie!

Mermaids dance beneath the waves,
With bubbles popping like giggly knaves.
Each wave a tale, each ripple a song,
In this watery world, I feel I belong.

## Stories Written in Sand

Sandcastles rise with a proud little grin,
While waves rush in to nibble their skin.
I draw cartoons with my toes in the sand,
Quickly erased by the tide's eager hand.

Children laugh as they play tag with the foam,
The ocean whispers, 'Let this be your home.'
With each grain falling, a tale to be spun,
Of pirate dreams and laughs in the sun.

## Voices from the Abyss

Bubbles whisper secrets loud,
Fish wear crowns, they swim so proud.
Octopus dreams of a fancy car,
Shark hums tunes from a distant bar.

Jellyfish dance in a wobbly throng,
Seahorses strut like they belong.
Crabs host parties on sandy floors,
Turtle takes bets on who's the slowest of four.

**Pelagic Patterns of Time**

Waves roll in like a giant dog,
Starfish stuck in a seaweed bog.
Clams throw shade on the passing fish,
As dolphins line up for a group photo wish.

Seagulls squawk out a silly tune,
While plankton hide from a curious moon.
Mermaids giggle at the barnacle's joke,
As sea cucumbers ponder, "Do we even poke?"

## **Silent Currents of History**

Turtles tell tales of lost treasure maps,
While eels play poker with sailor's caps.
Starry night brings tales from the reefs,
As conch shells giggle at the world's beliefs.

Barnacles form a council of sorts,
Debating if whales have the best reports.
Every clam holds a history grudge,
But no one dares to give them a nudge.

## The Unfolding Nautical Tale

A crab with a hat tells jokes by the shore,
While fishes giggle, always wanting more.
Octopus juggles with eight wiggly arms,
Pulling in crowds with his quirky charms.

Surfboards drift by in the ocean's laugh,
With dolphins taking selfies, what a gaff!
Even the plankton wear tiny berets,
In the underwater world, it's all play, hey!

## Waves Whispering Secrets

The waves gossip softly and sway,
Sharing tales from the light of day.
Fish in tuxedos, shrimps in a tie,
Making a splash as they pass by.

A crab in a hat, feeling quite proud,
Boasts of the treasure he found in the crowd.
Seagulls are laughing, a comedic sight,
As they dive for snacks, oh what a flight!

## **Echoes Beneath the Tide**

Beneath the surface, fish tell a joke,
Witty and sharp like a clever bloke.
A sardine slips, with a splash and a grin,
While clams hide their pearls, hoping to win.

Seaweed dances, a tangled delight,
Tickling the fins of a dolphin's flight.
Even the octopus, clever and sly,
Laughs at the fishermen passing by.

## Beneath the Ocean's Veil

Anemones wave like they're at a ball,
Inviting the guests for a wacky crawl.
Turtles wear glasses, looking so wise,
Count fish as they swim, what a surprise!

Starfish salute with their five little arms,
While clownfish bombard with their goofy charms.
The jellyfish bounce like they're on a spree,
Dancing through currents, wild and free!

## Currents of Forgotten Tales

In riptides of laughter, stories unfold,
Whales sing ballads from ages of old.
Octopus grins, with tricks up his sleeve,
Making shells giggle, what webs they weave!

Bubbles burst forth, a giggling parade,
As schools of fish join in the charade.
A lobster in shades, living so grand,
Cracks jokes with a wink and a wave of his hand.

## Lighthouses of the Past

Once stood bright, a guiding light,
Telling sailors, 'Take a right!'
But the seagulls had a laugh,
They took a turn, went for a bath.

Old towers wear a coat of rust,
Waving gently, 'In waves we trust.'
With a wink, they spin and sway,
While fish joke, 'We're on our way!'

## **Whispering Waters**

Whispers bubble from the deep,
'Swim with us, come take a leap!'
But the fish preferred to pout,
'We're too busy swimming about!'

Crabs tell tales of ships that sank,
Mollusks giggle at a prank.
'Oh, what fun they do not see,
We've parties 'neath the briny spree!'

## Echoes from the Abyss

Echoes rise from ocean floors,
Sea creatures laugh, 'We're such great shores!'
A whale sings with gravelly tone,
While turtles dance, 'We've found our bone!'

Bubbles burst like giggles loud,
Jellyfish sway, oh aren't they proud?
'Here's a riddle,' the octopus shrieked,
'Why's a clam so well-discreeked?'

## **Beneath the Surface**

Beneath the waves, a silly show,
Fish wear hats and dance with dough.
Crabs tap feet in fancy shoes,
While dolphins joke, 'We've got the blues!'

Anemones sway, in laughter bloom,
'Watch your step, make sure there's room!'
The seaweed sways to a rhythmic beat,
'Join our jam, get up on your feet!'

## Memories in a Jellyfish's Glow

In a dance of luminescence, quite absurd,
A jellyfish swirls, wisdom unheard.
It floats with a grin, what does it know?
Whispers of silliness in every glow.

A crab's on the run, with shoes too tight,
He trips on the sand and takes flight!
The seaweed chuckles, the fish roll their eyes,
As the tide tells tales, and no one denies.

Seagulls above sing an off-key tune,
While dolphins perform, all under the moon.
With laughter that bubbles in frothy waves,
The ocean holds secrets that none can save.

So if you should visit this watery realm,
Find humor and joy at the ocean's helm.
For in each ripple, silliness beams,
Locked in the laughter of saltwater dreams.

## Coral Beneath the Surface

Beneath the waves, where the coral lies,
A fish with odd glasses eyes the skies.
It's reading a book that weighs quite a ton,
"Underwater Chronicles of Fun!"

A turtle trots by, his shell all adorned,
With bumper stickers that leave one scorned.
He winks at a shrimp for a candid shot,
"Most stylish, you think?" It asks with a thought.

An octopus juggles with flair and finesse,
With eight tiny balls, making quite the mess.
The crowd of sea creatures bursts into glee,
As the sea anemones sway wildly with glee.

So listen closely, those down in the deep,
Echoes of giggles in currents they keep.
For with every splash, a chuckle will rise,
From the coral's laughter and fish's surprise.

## Castaways of the Current

Drifting along the current's embrace,
A sailor with locks that laugh in his face.
He's got a parrot that's lost all its charms,
Pulling off tricks with comical arms.

A castaway claims he's a pirate of old,
With a treasure map made of sandwich gold.
"Follow the crumbs!" he gleefully shouts,
As the ocean waves chuckle and roundabout sprout.

Starfish audition for some silly roles,
While clams in their shells call out for patrols.
"Don't leave us here!" they dramatically cry,
As sailors debate if they should fly high.

So float on the waves where the laughter runs free,
In the goofy world of the wild, open sea.
For every twist in the current you face,
Is a chance for a smile, an embrace of grace.

## Ghostly Sailors' Lament

Beneath the moon, with a spooky swish,
Ghostly sailors sing of their favorite dish.
"Did someone say fish?" one phantom did say,
While the others laughed and danced in dismay.

Their ship, once stout, now made of mist,
Its rusty old anchor had gone amiss.
With each eerie note, they twist and they twirl,
While gulls overhead give a disappointed whirl.

They reminisce about days at sea,
Where they never stashed snacks for tea.
"Unfinished adventures!" they howl with delight,
Under the stars, in the dark of the night.

So if you observe from the shore with a sigh,
Join in the fun with a wink of your eye.
For the dead droll sailors still know how to play,
With laughter as buoyant as a bright sunny day.

## Waves Carrying Forgotten Tales

Waves whisper secrets, oh so bold,
Stories of fish and sailors old.
A crab once danced, in salty glee,
Claiming the plankton as its tea.

Seagulls squawk, they steal the show,
Trying to juggle while on the go.
A shrimp played cards with a fishy foe,
"Five o'clock tide, let's make it a flow!"

## Remnants of a Distant Horizon

On shore I found a flip-flop shoe,
An odd reminder of something true.
It must have danced beneath the sun,
With waves as partners, oh what fun!

A bottle rolled in, holding a note,
"Help, I'm stuck with a rubber boat!"
Its journey long, so far to roam,
Seeking shores that it can call home.

## The Depths Remember

Down below, the fish hold court,
In fancy hats, at their seaweed sport.
A dolphin jokes, with a splash and spin,
"Who knew sea life could wear such fin?"

Turtles debate who's the best diver,
While octopuses serve as the provider.
The clownfish laughs, "I'm funny, you see!
Best at both comedy and being free!"

## Tides of Nostalgia

The tide rolls back with a cheerful hum,
Leaving behind a beach ball's drum.
It's played with shells and bits of foam,
Creating laughter, where sea creatures roam.

Just yesterday, a lobster's ballet,
Twisting and turning, in a clay-like sway.
The sand giggles where memories lie,
As the waves toss tales and bids goodbye.

## Castaway Echoes

A crab's dance on the shore, what a sight,
He wiggles like he's lost his last fight.
A bottle floats by, with a note so neat,
It says, 'Help! I'm lost! Where's my last treat?'

Seagulls squawking, they steal all the fries,
While dolphins are laughing, with mischievous eyes.
A sailor slips up, he falls with a splash,
His shipmates all giggle, oh what a crash!

The fish whisper tales of a boat made of cheese,
Where mermaids throw parties and serve ocean breeze.
A treasure chest found, but it's full of old shoes,
Who knew that the sea likes to play with our blues?

So here on the shore, we laugh and we cheer,
For every wild tale that the waves might hear.
With memories buried in deep ocean beds,
It seems even fish have their fun with our heads!

## **The Lament of Rusted Anchors**

Oh, the sad plight of anchors, stuck in the mud,
Once great ships trusted, now just a dud.
They rust and they moan, whisper tales of their past,
Like old sailors grumbling, about sails that won't last.

Once they held fast when storms brewed at night,
Now they just dream of their glorious flight.
They reminisce tales about their grand sails,
While gulls squawk in laughter, their humor prevails.

A barnacle jokes, 'Why don't you just float?'
The anchor replies, 'I'm stuck, don't you gloat!'
So they share the ocean, these friends who can't roam,
In a world full of waves, they've made their own home.

Still, they keep watch, with their rusted old chains,
While the fish flip 'round, collecting old gains.
To those who forget, they'll forever remind,
Of ships that once sailed, leaving memories behind!

# Whispers from the Drown

Deep in the depths where the bubbles collide,
Are tales of the sailors who took quite a ride.
With fish in tuxedos and seaweed attire,
They toast to the blunders of man's great desire.

A sailor's lost boot, now an octopus throne,
He rules with a laugh, his reign all alone.
The mermaids pass notes, like school kids in class,
About ships that sank fast, and the treasures they'd amass.

The anchors, they grumble, they'd rather be free,
Than listen to fish joke about old history.
But deep down they know, as they dwell in the foam,
That laughter's the treasure that's found in the loam.

So raise up your cups, made of coral and sand,
To the whispers of oceans, the best in the land.
For even in depths where the tragedy's found,
The jesters of water make laughter abound!

## Nautical Chronicles

Ahoy! Gather 'round for a story so grand,
Of swabs who got lost on a bright desert sand.
They thought they were sailors, so brave and so bold,
Until they found out, they had rocks, not gold!

With maps made of jelly and compasses wrong,
They followed a dolphin who sang them a song.
'You wanted the sea?' he laughed with a flip,
'You're lost in the desert! Now get back on your ship!'

The mermaids were puzzled, as their hair flowed gold,
"Why not join us? Here the water's not cold!"
But the pirates just sighed, with a laugh and a fight,
For who knew that desert would steal all their light?

So back in the ocean, where the sea breezes blow,
They'll tell of adventures only fish seem to know.
With tales of the desert, and a ship made of cheese,
Laughter turned waves, oh, with so much to please!

## Forgotten Shores

On sandy patches, lost shoes lay,
A crab in them, making a stay.
Seagulls laugh with a cheeky squawk,
While beach balls perform a wobbly walk.

Old boats grin, with paint all peeled,
Their stories told, though none revealed.
Fish in schools play tag with doom,
While splashes echo in the afternoon.

Tanned tourists chase their hats on air,
While sandcastles lose their regal flair.
A jellyfish floats by, wearing a crown,
As kids debate if it's up or down.

On shorelines dotted with half-eaten snacks,
Life's a circus, no one looks back.
With each wave's tickle, smiles so wide,
The ocean giggles, it's quite the ride.

## Dances of Driftwood

Driftwood logs in silly ranks,
Have more moves than average pranks.
They twist and twirl on the beachside floor,
While spectators laugh and call for more.

Old boots and flip-flops join the show,
With great ambition, they try but 'whoah!'
A splash and a wobble, then off they fly,
As the tide giggles and waves goodbye.

A bottle caps its boogie spree,
Wobbling about in pure glee.
As crabs breakdance, back-to-back,
While seagulls honk a catchy track.

The sun sets down on this grand ball,
With waves that ripple, in a joyful call.
As driftwood dreams of twirling all night,
The ocean applauds in gleeful delight.

## The Abyss Remembers

In deep blue halls where laughter fades,
With fishy tales that never jade.
Octopus chefs flip cuisine with flair,
While turtles giggle with splendid air.

Mermaids gossip, with scales that gleam,
Trading stories of an underwater dream.
But wait! What's that? A whale's blown a joke,
As bubbles rise, everyone's bespoke.

Treasure chests with old tunes ring,
As the sunken crowns begin to sing.
'What fun it is, to remember the laughs!'
Said a crab, while he juggled his halves.

And in the shadows, shy anemones,
Chuckled softly at all of these pleas.
With currents carrying joyful threads,
The ocean's giggle never dreads.

## Where Water Meets Whisper

Where the waves play peek-a-boo,
Whispers tickle the shoreline too.
A sandpiper dances, loses its shoes,
While seashells conspire with colorful hues.

Frothy laughter, that's what they claim,
As beachgoers join in the playful game.
'What did the wave say to the sand?'
'Let's stick together, it's oh so grand!'

A crab complains of a sidestep dance,
While fish sway with a watery prance.
A washed-up sock joins in the fun,
Realizing beach time's never done.

The horizon blushes with sunset's glow,
As whispers and giggles begin to flow.
For where water meets a playful cheer,
Laughter echoes, bringing joy near.

## The Lure of Lost Anchors

There once was a pirate, so bold and brash,
Whose treasure was lost in a bubble and splash.
He searched the deep blue with a map in his hand,
But all he found was a rusty old can.

His parrot would squawk, 'You're digging too deep!'
While he fished for sunken gold in waters so steep.
But each nugget he found was a piece of old toast,
And the laughing gulls called him their lost anchor host.

He'd argue with fishes and barter with crabs,
Over shiny old trinkets and mysterious jabs.
Yet they all just swam off with a flick of the tail,
Leaving him with soggy socks and a spluttering sail.

At last, with a sigh, he threw overboard thought,
And danced with the waves, a strange joy he sought.
For the treasures of laughter were plenty, it seemed,
In the ocean of nonsense where funny dreams streamed.

**Timeless Salted Stories**

A clam with a tale sat under the sun,
Claiming he'd once made a whale laugh and run.
With a shell full of giggles and pearls of delight,
He regaled every crab with his stories all night.

The octopus winked, with eight arms all aglow,
'Your tales are just tall, like the tide, they ebb slow!'
But the clam just chuckled, 'You're jealous, I see,
My legends are salted, like snacks, full of glee!'

With fish in the background who swam and who cheered,
The clam kept on spinning his yarns, never steered.
'Remember the time I bested a shark,
With nothing but humor, like throwing a lark?'

As the sun dipped low and the party grew bright,
The sea critters laughed 'til they lost all their might.
For sometimes the best, when it comes to the sea,
Are not just the waves, but the giggles they free.

## When Waves Remember

The ocean's giggle is a sound from the past,
Where each little wave has a story to cast.
They whisper of sailors lost in the foam,
With mismatched socks and a boat made of chrome.

Oh, the surf does chuckle at silly old tales,
Of mistimed nets and fish that wore scales.
A captain who thought he could dance on the shore,
And ended up tangled in seaweed galore!

The dolphins all joined in a watery jest,
With flips and with flops, at their very best.
'You'd think they'd have learned from the fish that they caught,
That schadenfreude is really quite silly and hot!'

But with every wave, they forgot and they played,
A memory dissolving, like laughter it swayed.
For the ocean knows well, in its bubbly embrace,
That funny is timeless, and troubles lose face.

## Faded Maps of Drifted Dreams

In a bottle once passed, there lay a small map,
With directions to find the best fish-flop trap.
The pirates all giggled, 'How ludicrous this!'
Yet they followed it anyway, chased by a kiss.

Through storms and through squalls, they sailed like mad fools,
With hopes for a bounty gold-lined with jewels.
But all they discovered was a tattered old shoe,
And a treasure of laughter that washed up anew.

'Are we lost?' one asked, as the seagulls went wild,
While the ocean just chuckled, its waves gently smiled.
They danced through the tides with a raucous delight,
Trading tales of lost futures and stars in the night.

So when they returned to the shore, full of cheer,
They realized the riches were never held dear.
For memories and giggles, like fine summer cream,
Were the wealth of their journey, their drifted-up dream.

## Memories Written in Currents

The fish in their hats swim around,
Doing the waltz without a sound.
Seagulls gossip, oh what a spread,
While turtles laugh at stories long dead.

Crabs carry phones, take selfies galore,
Who knew such chatter exists at the shore?
The waves recite tales, don't spill a drink,
As barnacles giggle and starfish wink.

The seaweed dances to songs made of salt,
While barnacle bouncers call 'no more malt!'
Whales tell jokes, their punchlines quite deep,
As ships sail by with secrets to keep.

In the realm of the waves, a show never ends,
As dolphins dive in with all of their friends.
A splash here, a splash there, laughter resounds,
In this watery world, joy endlessly bounds.

## From the Depths of Solitude

An octopus plays chess with a clam,
While sea cucumbers laugh at the jam.
The jokes they share, so silly, so grand,
Even the rocks rise up to withstand.

A lonely crab writes poems in sand,
With seafoam ink, it's all quite unplanned.
Jellyfish float with a whimsical grace,
As they make faces, it's all a race!

The tides tell riddles, quite hard to decode,
While shells spin yarns of stories bestowed.
In patches of sea, drama unfolds,
As fish swim round, striking poses so bold.

In solitude's depths, the laughter flows free,
Among quirky creatures, wild as can be.
With whiskers and fins, they dance and they spin,
In bubbles of joy, where the fun can begin.

## The Call of Distant Shores

A crab in a top hat hails a fine boat,
With sailors who can't seem to find their coat.
They venture forth, a motley crew,
Off to seek treasures, quite old and quite new.

The gulls squawk loud, like raucous cheer,
As seaweed sways, whispering, 'Come near!'
Fishes in tuxedos throw a grand ball,
While clams sing opera, not shy at all!

As tides ebb and flow, laughter intertwines,
Through voyage and regale, the fun truly shines.
With giggles and splashes, they sail to explore,
In search of good times along every shore.

Where waves carry whispers and secrets delight,
The calls of the ocean ring out through the night.
With hearts full of joy from the humor they find,
To distant horizons, they leave all behind.

## **A Storycarved in Coral**

In coral castles, the parties abound,
With clownfish jesters that dance all around.
They tickle the bubbles, play hide and seek,
While sea sponges giggle with every little squeak.

A seahorse DJ spins tunes from the sea,
Crabs on the dance floor have endless glee.
Starfish throw confetti, oh what a sight,
While turtles groove slowly, hearts full of light.

The coral holds tales of capers and whims,
Of shipwrecked tales told in joyful trims.
Echoes of laughter, like waves, roll and swell,
In the depths, every creature has stories to tell.

With wrinkled old shells, wisdom is shared,
As bubbles rise up, reminders of dared.
In this storybook world, where fun reigns supreme,
Each color, each dance is a whimsical dream.

## The Horizon's Silent Songs

The horizon sings a quirky tune,
With dolphins dancing to the moon.
Seagulls squawk in silly glee,
Whispering secrets, just for me.

The waves tickle boats like they're old friends,
Where laughter splashes, the fun never ends.
Fish flip-flop, trying to fly,
While crabs play cards, oh me, oh my!

Bubbles rise with a giggling sound,
Sandy feet race all around.
A treasure chest filled with socks and stones,
Underwater jokes make silly tones.

Here's to the jesters of the briny deep,
Where octopuses juggle, and starfish leap.
The horizon whispers, loud and bright,
In this goofy world, we sail with delight.

**Beneath the Surface Lies History**

Under the waves, the tales unfold,
Of pirates lost and treasures bold.
A fish in a hat, a whale with a grin,
History's humor where legends begin.

A shipwrecked galleon, what a sight!
With crabs hosting parties both day and night.
Mermaid gossip, oh what a riot,
Underwater life feels like a quiet diet.

Coral reefs, they giggle and sway,
As the ocean's jester makes fun every day.
Old sunken boats sharing a snicker,
While sea turtles navigate, oh so slicker!

With every tide, a new joke is cast,
History laughs, and the molds are amassed.
Dive beneath, and you might just see,
The whims of the ocean, wild and free.

# Waters Woven with Time

In waters woven with tales so fine,
A fish slips by, wearing a vine.
The turtles debate the best dance moves,
As the current giggles, and the wave grooves.

Ripples whisper secrets, oh so sly,
A pirate's hat floating up high.
Bubble parties with barnacles galore,
Every splash is a laugh that we adore.

The tides toss jokes like beach balls around,
While jellyfish shimmer with quirkiness bound.
A sea cucumber chuckles, stuck to a rock,
While octopuses prank, and everybody mocks.

The salty breeze carries laughter anew,
As crabs throw a shindig in bright ocean blue.
The waters weave memories, happy and light,
In this comical world, everything's right.

## The Boat With No Name

A boat with no name, adrift in the foam,
Holds fantasies wild, a seafarer's home.
It sails on a whim, with a laugh and a cheer,
While fish play the banjo, oh what a year!

With wind in its sails, it darts to and fro,
Telling tall tales of the ocean below.
A parrot recites rhymes out of tune,
As the stars wink down, and the night bathes in June.

It rocks with the rhythm of the ocean's jest,
Where mermaids hold court, and everyone's blessed.
A cabin of chuckles, a deck of delight,
In the boat with no name, the fun takes flight!

So here's to the adventures on waves we embrace,
With a bow that won't bow to the mundane race.
Life's a riddle on this ship so tame,
Boundless laughter—forever the aim!

## Lament of the Lapping Waves

Waves come in with playful glee,
Bringing tales of fish and spree.
They whisper jokes on sandy shores,
Of sunburnt tourists and ice cream wars.

Seagulls squawk in lively chatter,
While crabs dance in a silly patter.
Shells giggle when they catch a breeze,
Remembering when they were part of keys.

The tide rolls in with a sneaky grin,
Swapping secrets where laughter's been.
Each splash tells tales that no one sees,
Of mermaids' quirks and jellyfish knees.

Oh, the ocean's a trickster, it seems,
Wearing a hat adorned with dreams.
It knows the dance of each sunlit ray,
Laughing as it rolls away!

## Memories in Salt and Brine

In salty air, the memories swirl,
Of fishy tales and seaweed twirl.
The sands have stories—some absurd,
Like a clam that fancied itself a bird.

A dolphin once tried to juggle fish,
Declaring it his secret wish.
But alas, the fishy fleet just flopped,
And in the laughter, they all dropped.

Tide pools hide the silliest sights,
Tiny crabs dressed up for fights.
Each ripple holds a giggle and grin,
Echoing laughter captured within.

Salted forget-me-nots drift and sway,
The ocean's giggles steal the day.
If only we knew what they might say,
As we bask in their whimsical play!

## The Fluidity of Remembrance

Oh, waves, you quirky, wavy friends,
Carrying giggles until the end.
Each splash seems to chime and sing,
Of seahorses dressed as queens in spring.

Ebbing tides with a chuckle loud,
Bringing back tales beneath the cloud.
A starfish struts with a jaunty flair,
While turtles tell puns that float in air.

The dolphins, who moonlight as jesters bright,
Play fishy pranks well into the night.
They juggle bubbles, roll and dive,
As all the corals laugh and thrive.

So here's to the tide that leaves us grinning,
With jokes and jests forever spinning.
Each wave a wink, each tide a cheer,
In this vibrant world where joy is near!

## Shells of Yesterday

Shells on the shore hold giggles old,
Each one a story just waiting to be told.
The snails narrate in whispers soft,
Of blustery winds and seagulls aloft.

Crabs clink glasses at twilight's fall,
Posing for selfies, they have a ball.
Clibbity-clop, they scurry with flair,
In the memory dance of ocean's fair.

Mollusks chat with a hint of sass,
Riffing on life and fishes that pass.
Each wave a reminder, each tide a jest,
Of salty shenanigans, they like best!

With laughter echoing through sand and foam,
These shells certainly call ocean their home.
A treasure chest of whimsy, delight,
In the heart of the waves, a wondrous sight!

## Ocean's Oldest Chronicles

The fish all gather round with glee,
To share the tales of Captain Glee.
His socks he lost in a mighty squall,
And how he slipped, oh what a fall!

The jellyfish can't stop their laugh,
As they recount his silly gaffe.
With every wave, more stories swell,
Of ocean blunders that they tell.

Even the crabs are in on the fun,
Chasing each other in a race to run.
But every time they're close to win,
One trips and goes back to the fin.

So come and listen to the tale,
Of fishy pranks in the briny gale.
Beneath the waves, joy reigns supreme,
In the chronicles of an ocean dream.

## The Riddle of the Reefs

Oh the coral asks, what likes to dive?
A sardine squad, all smiles alive.
They flutter and flit through waters bright,
In search of mysteries, day and night.

A sea turtle claims to hold the truth,
His wisdom sneaks up like missing tooth.
But all he knows is where to nap,
While searching for the snack—oh, snap!

The urchins laugh with prickly delight,
As waves push tales of fishy spite.
"Why did the tuna cross the bay?
To get to the other side, I say!"

So riddles twist in ocean's sway,
With laughter echoing in their play.
The reefs are filled with jokes aplenty,
And secrets locked like treasure, gently.

## Whispers of the Tidal Past

Shells hold whispers of days gone by,
With tales so funny they make you cry.
The octopus wore a pirate's hat,
And danced with a crab—imagine that!

Anemones giggle with colorful flair,
Watching fish trip in comedic despair.
Swim, swim, whoops! Down goes a grouper,
And up pops a sardine, yelling 'scooper!'

Whispers twirl like bubbles in air,
Of fishy fights and jellycare.
"Why swim away?" the clownfish joked,
"It's just a wave, don't be provoked!"

So listen close when the tide retreats,
For laughter lingers in watery beats.
The sea's a stage where comedians play,
In the rhythms of night, in the dance of day.

## Echoes Beneath the Waves

Echoes drift in every tide,
Where fishes laugh and seahorses glide.
"Did you hear?" a whale would bellow,
Of a clam that thought he was a jello!

Dolphins giggle with flips and spins,
Competing with seals, who've got their fins.
"What's a sea's favorite game of chance?
'Go Fish!' they sang, in a lively dance!"

The eels, in rhythm, dance and shout,
Heckling the lobsters without a doubt.
"Don't pinch your pals, that's so passé,
Just wave your arms and dance away!"

So as the bubbles rise and fall,
Dive deep to hear the ocean's call.
With every echo, find some cheer,
In the laughter of water, bright and clear.

## Ocean's Forgotten Lore

In tidal waves of jellyfish,
A sailor lost his trusty dish.
He swore it danced and serenely glowed,
But really it just floated—oh what a load!

The dolphins played a game of tag,
While seagulls squawked—what a rag!
One finned friend slipped on a shell,
And rolled away, oh what a swell!

Turtles wearing silly hats,
Joined in chorus with the cats.
A fish with glasses read a book,
While crabs all peeked from their nook.

So raise a glass, a toast to cheer,
For the ocean's tales, let's keep them near!
With laughter echoing through the tide,
In every wave, a secret hides.

## Fables from Coral Caverns

In caverns bright, where clowns do dance,
The lobsters join, they take a chance.
A shrimp told jokes, a crab laughed loud,
While starfish spun, oh, what a crowd!

Octopuses inked their own reviews,
On underwater humor and daily blues.
A mackerel wore a polka-dot tie,
And asked a whale—why is the sky?

The clams held court with goofy glee,
While clownfish swam up to thee.
They swapped their tales of lost sock,
And how they lost it on a rock!

With bubbles bursting in delight,
These fables sparkled, oh so bright.
From coral homes, the laughter swells,
In the deep, where humor dwells.

## Nautical Whispers

A whisper floats from brine so deep,
Of mermaids who in silence weep.
But when they giggle, oh what a sight,
They tickle fish till it's late at night!

The anchors groan in tired moans,
As barnacles sing their silly tones.
A seagull dropped a sandwich too,
Reeling back, he plotted his coup.

The buoys bob up with quite the flair,
Holding secrets beyond compare.
They gossip low in buoyant tones,
About the dolphin's latest loans!

In ripples soft, the tales unfold,
With humor warm, and legends bold.
So keep your ears by the shore,
For whispers that make the sea roar!

## Ghostly Breaths of the Abyss

In shadows where the eels do glide,
A ghostly fish takes a chummy ride.
He tells of treasures that never were found,
Where pirates just left their socks on the ground!

Smooth rocks giggle under the chill,
As the crab's dance gives the sea a thrill.
An octopus jokes about his lost prize,
A rubber duck with very wide eyes!

With sounds like farts and bubbles of mirth,
They tease each other of ancient worth.
For in the depths, laughter does thrive,
In the eerie gloom, it's how we survive!

So lift your spirits, don't think of dread,
Where sea ghosts frolic, and laughter's widespread.
In the abyss, with shadows and gleam,
Frolic and dance in the watery dream!

## Serpentine Shores and Echoing Memories

On serpentine shores, where crabs do dance,
The seagulls squawk, giving fish a chance.
A tide of laughter, waves in a race,
Shells gossip softly, with a wink on their face.

Bulls of waves crash with comical flair,
Starfish stuck, looking for a spare chair.
With jellyfish jiggles under the sun,
Every splash and tumble, just silly fun.

Flip-flops are flying, as kids leap about,
Sandcastles crumble, oh what a rout!
A beach ball bounces, right into Dad's hat,
The ocean giggles, "Oh, imagine that!"

Seashells collect tales of laughter and cheer,
While dolphins are plotting their next big steer.
The tide rolls in, with memories to find,
And we laugh with the ocean, our hearts intertwined.

**Old Songs of the Brine**

The brine sings out with a chorus of cheer,
With fishy old tales that tickle the ear.
A crab playing violin on a rock,
While octopuses tap dance and squawk.

The gulls join in with a squawk and a swoop,
While turtles keep time in a gooey loop.
Under the sun, they all take a bow,
Salty serenades, oh wow, wow, wow!

Rusty old anchors hum out of tune,
With barnacles drumming a carefree croon.
The flip of a fin, and a splashy surprise,
Old songs come alive, 'neath wide-open skies.

With laughter like waves, rolling in and out,
The memories swirl in a jubilant shout.
Oh, old songs of brine, we'll cherish your sound,
While the ocean chuckles, swirling all around.

## A Palette of Oceanic Pastels

In a palette bright, where colors collide,
The ocean's artwork brings joy, not pride.
Pink fish in stripes do a wiggly dance,
While corals giggle, giving critters a chance.

Pastel clouds float with a playful breeze,
And sea turtles drift 'round, aiming to tease.
The starfish tosses seaweed like confetti,
While crabs throw their shells, all simmered and petty.

A splash from a porpoise breaks the play,
While jellyfish glide, in a graceful display.
With laughter like bubbles, they rise to the sky,
An art show from nature, oh me, oh my!

So grab your sun hat, let's wander the shore,
Among vibrant hues, we can't help but explore.
The ocean's a canvas, so vibrant and grand,
Reminiscing in laughter, hand in hand.

## Beneath the Foamy Veil

Beneath the foam, where giggles convene,
Barnacles chatter, with tales unseen.
The starry-eyed fish wear glasses of glass,
While dolphins rehearsed for their next big class.

The waves tease the shore, with a wiggle and taunt,
As crabs pull their best "look at me" stunt.
With seaweed wigs on their shiny old heads,
They shimmy and shake as they chat in their beds.

The tide ebbs and flows, with playful delight,
Sea cucumbers giggle at ghost crabs in flight.
A sandpiper trips, then laughs at the scene,
While clams roll their eyes at the chaos routine.

Under the veil where the lighthouse beams bright,
The ocean's a stage for our joyful delight.
So come join the fray, let the laughter unveil,
In a world full of whimsy, beneath the white veil.

## Salty Remnants of Yesteryears

Once a crab wore a monocle,
Thinking he was quite dandy.
He danced on a sandy stage,
To impress a shrimp so handy.

Seagulls squawked with delight,
Trading stories of old fish tales.
One claimed to have met a mermaid,
Who flipped a boat with her scales.

Turtles wearing funky hats,
Strolled along the foamy shore.
Debating if they should swim,
Or catch a wave and just snore.

In the silence, a clam giggled,
Singing about a wave's great crash.
While starfish played a game of cards,
With a dazzling, colorful splash.

## Chronicles of the Ocean Depths

A fish dreamed of being a poet,
But his rhymes were all quite fishy.
He wrote of bubbles and tides,
And of a crab who got squishy.

Octopus set up a market,
For treasures lost long ago.
Offering pearls to the gulls,
But nobody wanted the show.

The jellyfish in a tutu,
Glided past, oh so fancy.
Proclaiming her jelly reign,
With a dance quite so chancy.

Meanwhile, clowns in the coral,
Juggled clams with a grin.
For what's a show in the depths,
If you can't tease a fin?

**Ghosts of Sailors Long Gone**

Whispers of sailors extend,
Riddled with laughter and cheer.
Tales of fish hooking their hats,
And a ship that drank all their beer.

A captain once lost his wig,
To a storm that was quite a tease.
He swore it swam for the horizon,
Leaving him with a chilly breeze.

The crew threw sausage parties,
Invited the lobsters and crabs.
But the crustaceans always left,
Claiming they were too fab.

Now they haunt the salty breezes,
With their tales of grand old fun.
Dancing in the moonlit waves,
As if they've never been done.

## **Secrets Buried in the Blue**

Beneath the waves lies a treasure,
Of old shoes and rusty spoons.
Mermaids giggle in delight,
As they dance with the low-tide moons.

An octopus holds a diary,
With pages that are quite damp.
Filled with seaweed gossip,
And a very flamboyant lamp.

Crabs search for buried secrets,
While dolphins shoot the breeze.
They chuckle at lost umbrellas,
That float with such swagger and ease.

If you listen to the bubbles,
You might hear the ocean's cheer.
It's filled with laughter and mischief,
And, of course, some wiggly fear.

## Remnants of Fathoms Past

In the depths where fish do play,
Old stories drift, then fade away.
A crab with glasses, reading the news,
As jellyfish dance in their fancy shoes.

Seashells gossip on the shore,
Of mermaids lost, and tuna wars.
A bubble bursts with laughter's cheer,
Echoes of whales who forgot their gear.

An octopus juggles a treasure chest,
While finding the map? Just a guess.
The anchor sighs, it feels so old,
Like tales of sailors, proudly told.

So let's raise a toast to the clam and the snail,
For every wave hides a curious tale.
In the ocean's laughter, we always swim,
Holding our sides as the tide grows dim.

## **Recollections of Celestial Waters**

Splashing reflections of starlit dreams,
Squid pen scribbles in shimmering streams.
A turtle in shades, oh so cool,
While eels play chess by the old coral pool.

Gulls cackle news from the peppered crust,
Of fishy friends and the crustacean trust.
They tickle the waves that are rolling in,
While seahorses giggle, their scales in a spin.

The pirate ship dances, its flag all a-flutter,
As dolphins yell jokes, with quite a loud utter.
The tide comes and goes, like a cheeky prank,
As starfish flip tales, right there on the plank.

So cast off your worries, let laughter prevail,
For in the deep blue, absurdity's sail.
Spin yarns with the crabs, oh what a delight,
In waters where memories twinkle so bright.

**Waves of Yore**

The waves keep secrets, they wiggle and swirl,
In a clam's quiet laugh, a curious pearl.
A fish in a top hat, what a sight to see,
Debating with seaweed on tea and the brie.

A sea cucumber floats, feeling quite spry,
While dolphins tell tales that could make you cry.
A plankton parade, tiny floats everywhere,
Disguised as confetti, they dance without care.

Sailors once sailed on a laugh and a prayer,
But now just rejoice in the salty sea air.
With each passing wave comes a tickling breeze,
Echoing laughter, like jokes from the seas.

So dive in the humor, the tides of pure fun,
Where mermaids play pranks and the currents all run.
In this world of mishaps and jesting at play,
We'll reminisce evenings, then splash the night away.

## A Journey in the Sea's Embrace

In the cradle of waves, where silliness brews,
The flounder wears spectacles, spreading the news!
With starfish as ushers and clams setting trends,
Each bubble a chuckle shared with all friends.

Anemones wiggle in carefree delight,
While crabs dance and salsa, oh what a sight!
The barnacles gossip like grandmas awake,
With tales of the sailors who've made quite a mistake.

Every splash tells a story of laughter and cheer,
Of toothy grins from the fish that appear.
The tide rolls in, and oh what a ride,
With sea cucumbers joining the fun far and wide.

So let's set our sails for the comedic tide,
With turtles on surfboards, oh what a glide!
In this vast ocean of giggles and grace,
We'll find a new journey in each salty space.

## Cavernous Memories of the Deep

Bubbles rise like whispers, so playful and bright,
Fish laugh in the shadows, quite the silly sight.
A treasure chest chuckles, full of coins that clink,
While an octopus winks and orders a drink.

A crab tells jokes, his pincers a-flap,
While starfish groove to the ocean's tap.
"Why did the clam take a nap?" he does tease,
"Because it wanted to snooze with the gentle breeze!"

Squid squirt ink like confetti in a stew,
Dancing with seaweed, they twirl just for you.
The kelp is a crowd, swaying left and right,
They giggle, they snort, what a coastal delight!

So next time you dip your toes in the foam,
Remember the laughter that calls it home.
For in watery depths, where the laughter roams free,
The memories murmur, "Come join the spree!"

## The Heartbeat of Sunken Dreams

A mermaid's serenade drifts through the tides,
She strums her shell guitar, and the fish all glide.
With each silly note, the barnacles dance,
While crabs in their best suits join the chance.

The ships that have sunk hold secrets untold,
Maybe a pirate's tales wrapped up in gold.
But all they discuss are jellyfish pranks,
And how sea turtles swim with clever old flanks.

A whale sings a hum that's cheerful and round,
As dolphins do flips and leap off the ground.
"Have you heard," they boast, "of the giant squid's plot?
He tried to bake cookies—what a twist and what not!"

In this underwater frolic, where laughter's the stitch,
Even sea cucumbers wiggle, oh what a hitch!
So come join the fun, let the currents be bold,
For the ocean's heartbeat whispers stories of old.

## Drifted Echoes

In the tide's gentle arms, echoes of fun,
A sea sponge tells tales of the places he's spun.
While seahorses giggle, wearing such flair,
With lashes so long, they could hand out some care.

Waves whisper secrets, soft as a breeze,
A clam flips a flap and begs to appease.
"Did you hear about bubbles that floated too high?
They went to a party, oh my, oh my!"

Anemones dance, with sprightly delight,
Embracing the currents, twirling in light.
Crabs in tuxedos go waltzing in pairs,
While jellyfish giggle, unpaired, with no cares.

These echoes of whimsy play hide and seek,
With seashells that chime and their laughter they leak.
In this watery world, always ready to play,
The drifted echoes invite you to stay!

## The Calm After Forgotten Storms

Once waves raged and howled, but now all is calm,
The fish share their stories, a soothing balm.
"Remember the gales?" says a flounder in jest,
"When the seashells had hats? Oh, that was the best!"

A faded old ship speaks of life on the run,
Of piratical parties, all in good fun.
"Why bury our treasure?" says a squid with a wink,
"When we could build castles and never go drink!"

With sea stars at play after wild winds have passed,
They flip and they laugh, oh what a contrast!
"Let's ride on the waves, let go of our fears,
And dance in the moonlight, with giggles and cheers!"

So let's heed the calm and cherish the sway,
For laughter is stronger than storms on the spray.
In this peaceful embrace, the ocean's a friend,
Where each giddy wave brings a smile to transcend.

## Saltwater Serenade

Waves that giggle, splash and play,
Crabs in costumes on a ballet.
Seagulls dive for stolen fries,
While fish swim by with big, round eyes.

Salty breezes tickle your nose,
In a treasure chest, a sock, it shows!
A dolphin winks, says, "What's the fuss?"
As my sunscreen turns me into a bus!

Sandcastles crumble, a humorous plight,
They topple over at the first sunlight.
Children scream, then burst into giggles,
As the tide comes in, and the sand wiggles.

In this concert of water and glee,
Even a pirate forgets how to be.
With laughter, the ocean calls us near,
Join the fun, let go of your fear!

## The Depths Remember

Bubbles float up, secrets upset,
Fish grinning at a pirate's pet.
A treasure chest filled up with shoes,
Oh, the tales those goofy crabs could choose!

Octopus dances in polka-dot suits,
With jellyfish friends, they form funky troupes.
A whale's loud laugh shakes the ocean blue,
While barnacles gossip with much ado!

Shells whisper stories of beach mischief,
Of towels lost in a windy cliff.
Sea turtles chuckle as they drift by,
"Remember that time? Oh my, oh my!"

In the depths, the humor never stops,
When eels tell jokes and the wave-laughter plops.
So dive on down, don't be shy or grumpy,
Join the fun where the currents are jumpy!

## **Recollections in Blue**

A rubber duck floats in endless sprawl,
A playful shark with a beach ball.
Mermaids giggle, tails in a twirl,
Swapping stories with a laughing pearl.

The sun wears shades, a floppy hat,
While starfish argue, "No, I'm not that fat!"
They trade their secrets, the tide rolls higher,
"Last week's swim was the real show- stopper!"

Fish arrange a comedy show,
With pufferfish acting as the star of the show.
"Knock, knock!" they say, "Who's swimming there?"
The seaweed laughs without a care.

So raise a glass of salty brine,
To the quirky tales, the jests that shine.
In this laughter, lost moments float,
Where every wave sings a funny note!

## **Nautical Ghosts**

Ghostly sailors, with giggles galore,
Haunting shipwrecks but craving more.
"Do you remember the crab's mime act?
It was a hit till the tide just cracked!"

Their old boats creak, making silly sounds,
As they dance to ethereal rounds.
With barnacles wearing sheet masks so bright,
They twirl and swirl in moonbeam light.

Mermaids shimmer, joining the fun,
While clams applaud, "More, more!" they run.
Cackling corpses in underwater play,
Sharing punchlines from their salty day.

So if you hear laughter in the foggy night,
Don't be afraid, it's just pure delight.
Nautical spirits, here to amuse,
In a world of giggles, they can't refuse!

## A Nautical Recollection

Once a crab wore a hat, so fine,
He danced on the sand, drank seawater wine.
The shells laughed and snickered, what a sight,
As seagulls cheered, 'What a marvelous night!'

A fish hired a shark for a timely trip,
Said, 'Dude, hold my fins, don't let it slip!'
They tumbled through waves, in a whirlpool play,
While dolphins took selfies, shouting 'Hey, hey!'

An octopus threw a grand tea party,
With jellyfish dancing, oh so tarty.
A turtle arrived, quite late and slow,
He grinned, 'I'm here! Now let's start the show!'

Then a walrus juggled seaweed with flair,
While clams played maracas, quite unaware.
The tide rolled in; laughter filled the breeze,
A memory made, as easy as cheese!

## The Ocean's Silent Archive

Under the waves, treasures piled high,
An old boot with tales and a fish that could fly.
A mermaid once lost her favorite comb,
Now it leads to a sunken, talking dome.

A parrotfish claimed he once saw the moon,
Danced with an eel to a jazzy tune.
They both giggled soft, then told silly lies,
As crabs cracked up with their subtle replies.

An anchor grew tired of holding the boats,
So he joined a band of rhythmic old goats.
They played their horns made of seashells and bones,
And shocked the sea urchins with humorous tones.

But then came a storm, all jigs turned to plight,
Yet laughter still echoed, despite the fright.
For in salty waters and waves of delight,
The tales keep on swimming, through day and through night.

## Currents of Lost Time

Remember when fish could dance on a line?
They'd wiggle and giggle, claiming it's fine.
A clam told a story so wonderfully grand,
That an ancient whale snorted, 'Oh, that's quite planned!'

A lighthouse decided to have a vacation,
And packed up a crab for a wild exploration.
As they traveled through fog, they got lost one day,
But it turned into fun, made a game of the fray.

Starfish threw parties under the moon,
While plankton recited a weird little tune.
The sea foam giggled, while twirling around,
As everyone danced to the ocean's sweet sound.

But time slipped away with the tide on its back,
Leaving behind memories, a quirky old stack.
Yet each wave that crashes, and every sweet chime,
Reminds us of laughter, in currents of time.

## Driftwood Diaries

A piece of driftwood thought it was grand,
Scribbled a tale with a splotchy hand.
It spoke of adventures with fish and with fowl,
And laughed with sea creatures, including a cow.

A seahorse read tales of a faraway lake,
Where frogs wore tuxedos and danced by a cake.
Fish chuckled so hard, they dropped their sweet snacks,
While crabs made a chorus with clever voice cracks.

Then came a whale with a grand, booming laugh,
Said, 'Don't be so silly, I'm here for the graph!'
He drew all the currents, the tides and the swells,
With stories of gossip, and tales of the shells.

But as night fell softly over waters so blue,
The driftwood just sighed, 'I've told all I knew.'
Yet in the moon's light, new tales still unfold,
In this ever-wet book, with laughter retold.

www.ingramcontent.com/pod-product-compliance
Lightning Source LLC
Chambersburg PA
CBHW060142230426
43661CB00003B/537